The Bright Red Book Of Happiness

Published by Philip Deal Books, LLC
Charlotte, North Carolina
philipdealbooks.com

ISBN 978-0615650111

This book is dedicated to my family and friends, who have made me smile, laugh, believe, hope, hug, cry, wonder, and desire.

Also By Philip Deal

Love In An Iron Bowl
OHM - A Novel of Resistance
Peculiar Hallelujah

THE BRIGHT RED BOOK
OF HAPPINESS

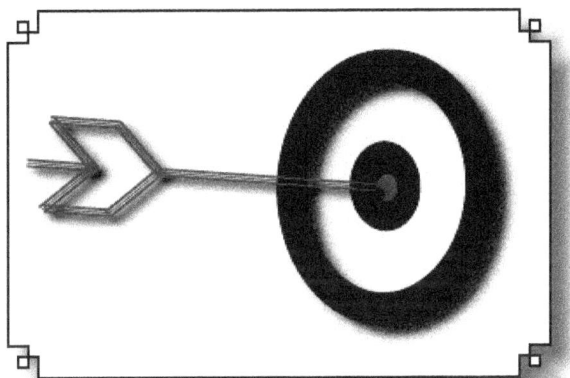

Table of Contents

Who The What? 1

Happiness Myths 6

Fully Automated 12

Welcome To Your Treadmill 24

Day 1 28

Night 1 32

Day 2 36

Green Marbles And Red Marbles 42

Day 1 Again 48

Day 2 Again 50

As Good As It Gets 56

Who You Want To Be 62

Getting There, Part One 72

Good-Byes 78

Getting There, Part Two 80

What To Expect Since You're Expecting 88

What Might Be Possible 94

Appendix: Questions You Can Use Right Now 100

Who the What?

This is me.

And this is me at different times in my life.

I show you these pictures for two reasons:

1. In case you picked up this book to find out if I am "that" Philip Deal.

The famous ballet dancer	NO
The instrumentalist who sometimes plays out his nose	NO
The English professor you knew at	
• Wichita State University	YES
• The Zhengzhou Aeronautics Institute	YES
• Georgia Southern University	YES

2. To show you that at different times in my life I have been thinner and fatter and older and younger and better and worse.

And while we're getting to know each other, here are a couple of other fun things to know about me:

I currently live in Charlotte, North Carolina, which, if we already knew each other, would be funny for a lot of reasons.

If I could do anything I wanted whenever I wanted, I would snorkel all day, then at night make photography books about undersea life.

So now you know three things that make me happy: snorkeling, photography, and writing.

WHO THE WHAT?

Which brings us to my credentials for writing **this** book. In the pages that follow, I'm going to ask you to think about how you ended up holding this book, and about how the choices you make as you read it have the power to radically alter your future. For that to work, you're going to have to trust me, and the fastest way to make that happen is to convince you that I'm a trustworthy author **for this particular book**. So here we go.

1. While some of my friends knew exactly what they would do after college, and some of them took one job just because they couldn't think of another, I have spent my entire life looking for ways to put happiness at the forefront of my existence. This has made my life interesting, fun, and difficult, sometimes all at the same time.

2. Although I started life as a fiery optimist, at some undefined moment in adulthood I slipped and fell. And then I slipped again. And then again. (This probably makes me a bit like you.) I have become a fiery optimist once more, and I am fairly certain I will stay that way the rest of my life. I tell you this so you will know that what I write about did not come automatically. I assure you that I have put in plenty of hard work. Find anyone who has been my friend for more than an hour and they will tell you that about me.

3. I have not always been as kind to others as I should have been, but I've also done some very nice things for people. I tell you this because it makes me human and worthy of your compassion.

4. I can be moody, and when I am I let little things bother me more than they should. This means I have to work very hard sometimes to control my moods. If you ask my wife I assure you she will tell you I am not always good at it. I tell you this about myself because I want you to know that being happy is not the same thing as being perfect. One of them is possible; the other is not.

5. I have lived all over the world and I have had a wide range of experiences, both personal and professional. I tell you this because I'm proud of it and wanted to brag.

6. This next one is very important. When I was 21 my Aunt Betty pointed out that I was trying to be perfect, and that I was therefore doomed to be miserable. Aunt Betty got this one exactly right. Since then I have a new mantra: Don't try to be perfect, just try to be happy. You're going to need the forgiveness of your loved ones anyway. If this sounds a bit like item number four, it probably is. I tell you this because some things are worth repeating.

7. Here are the rest of my credentials.

   I have two college degrees, one an M.F.A. in English, one a Bachelor's in Psychology.

   For ten years I tried to teach college students how to be better writers, which means I did my best to teach them how to be better thinkers.

   For ten years after that I developed something called "Learning" – twice in the Telecommunications industry (fun), once in the Financial Services industry (a disaster), and several times as an independent consultant (the only way to live in corporate America).

WHO THE WHAT?

I have succeeded and failed as a writer, a photographer, an artist, a teacher, a trainer, and a corporate escape artist. I tell you this so you'll know the obvious - I'm still trying to figure out what I want to be when I grow up.

I am a decent piano player, a fairly good cook, and in college I once burped the alphabet twice all the way through on a single burp (you can ask Brad Moore if you don't believe me). I tell you these things because they're more interesting to know about me than how old I am or how much I weigh.

I am happily married, and I have a wonderful daughter, who, if not for the insistent good sense of my wife (just one of the reasons I'm happily married), would have identical first and middle names.

I have written a few other books, some like this one, some completely different, some published, some unpublished, which I tell you for two reasons: 1) so you'll know this is not my first go at it, and 2) so you'll be curious enough to track down my other books after you've finished this one.

Chapter 1

Happiness Myths

writing myth   writing fact

These are the words my college writing students saw on the blackboard their first day of class each semester. Before I told them anything – the books they needed to buy, how I graded, or any of the other things I knew a lifetime of being a student had taught them to expect – I dove right into the writing myths I knew we would have to bury before they could start writing for real.

I tell this story now because there are some Happiness Myths we probably need to bury before we start talking about

happiness. Here are four of the most common ones.
You might want to hold onto something as you read.

HAPPINESS MYTHS

1. **MYTH: Happiness is the natural state of human beings. FACT:** Our natural state is wary alertness, which means being ready to do whatever we have to do to survive, and that's not the same as happiness. In fact, it's not even close. The good news is that as evolved beings we no longer have to live our entire lives in our natural state – we have the ability to imagine, to think for ourselves, and that gives us the ability to live lives that are much more enjoyable than lives lived entirely in our natural state.

2. **MYTH: Happiness is like a roaring fire that provides continuous warmth and joy. FACT:** Only if you do what's necessary to keep that fire burning. You have to break up your fire's embers, you have to re-adjust the position of your wood to let it breathe, you have to supply fresh wood to keep your flames burning. Ignore these requirements and your roaring fire will die – no matter how much you plead, pray, or beg for it to remain.

3. **MYTH: Happiness is an attainable final destination. FACT:** No matter how much you want your life to be that way, no matter how hard you work at it, no matter how many books you read – or for that matter write – you're never going to wake up one morning to

7

discover that you have no more work to do. There is no way to earn your happiness merit badge, pin it on your sash, then say *All done!*

4. **MYTH: Happiness is self-sustaining. FACT:** Happiness, it turns out, is a maintenance game. If you hope to remain happy – and there's really no reason to become happy unless you plan to stay that way – even more important than learning how to be happy is making a commitment to your maintenance game. Play your maintenance game well and happiness will be your lifelong friend. Become lackluster about that game and you run the risk of losing everything you've gained – no matter how hard you worked to get there.

Hmmm. Not all these facts are uplifting, and you're probably wondering how we're ever going to get from here to happiness. The great news is that each of us has a tool at our disposal that can't wait to get into the happiness game, and that tool is always nearby. It's not a book you read (including this one), or a philosophy you learn, or a religion you practice. It's the **actual** power of your **actual** mind to ask **actual** questions that direct your mind to do **actual** work for you. Ask the right questions, then get those questions up and running on their own, and you are well down the path of your choosing. All it takes is a little work.

Of course, that's the rub. To many people the idea of having to work to be happy is not only annoying, it seems all wrong. They believe that happiness is not something we should have to work our way into, over and over and over again, but something we just need to remember how to feel. After all, children are happy. Aren't they?

Yes, they are. But that doesn't matter. Because when we were children our path was laid out for us. Most of what we did each day was planned, and most of the time we did what we were told. When we were done doing what we were told, being happy came naturally to us. After all, we had no responsibilities, no important decisions to make, and no consequences of any consequence. So we played, and so we were, for the most part, happy. Spend half an hour at any playground and you'll see what I mean.

Adulthood, however, is a completely different ride. Things are no longer laid out for us. As adults we must **choose** how to spend our time. We **choose** the jobs we take. We **choose** to get married or to remain single, to have children, to scuba dive, to oil paint, to knit or join that bicycle club.

The distinction between a child's life of acting naturally and an adult's life of choosing is important, because it shows us that the path of our lives is not linear. **Adulthood is not an extension of youth**. Adulthood is a radical shift in how we spend our time, what we care about, what is expected from us, and - yes - how we find happiness. Gone are the days when we can wake up, put it on autopilot, then go out and play.

This means that as adults we need new tools for making ourselves happy, and that's why the four Happiness Myths are important. **Because they tell us exactly what we must do to be happy -**

1. We must work to make ourselves happy instead of letting wary alertness hold center stage (making us feel

edgy, nervous, and fearful, like an animal protecting its territory).

2. We must stoke our happiness flames as often as we can so they don't go out.

3. We must work at being happy instead of trying to find a nonexistent place to live called Happy Land.

4. We must develop a sensible and reasonable happiness maintenance plan so we don't have to spend all our time fighting and struggling.

The Bright Red Book of Happiness gives you a plan for making yourself happy and staying that way. The name of that plan is **The Fully Automated Treadmill Illumination Plan**. The next chapter introduces you to that plan. For now...

class dismissed

Chapter 2

Fully Automated

Three Years Ago	Right Now
Completely Inactive	Highly Active
A 215 pound blob	Healthy at 180-185
Ate chips & pizza	Still eat chips & pizza
Extremely moody	Moderately moody
Pessimistic	Highly Optimistic
Art projects collecting dust	Constantly making art

You might not believe me when I tell you this, but the way the guy on the left turned himself into the guy on the right is by committing to one – and to only one – idea:

I can do anything for two days.

And before I say another word I need to reveal the most important secret of **The Fully Automated Treadmill Illumination Plan**:

Doing anything for two days = Doing almost nothing

That's right, almost nothing. **Commit yourself to doing almost nothing for two days and you can make any change in your life that you want to make.** So while we're at it, let's nail that equation all the way down.

Doing anything for two days = Doing almost nothing =

Getting up thirty minutes early to work a change plan

Now if the idea of getting up early bothers you, take a minute to indulge yourself. I've even given you a bit of space below to do that. Go ahead. It's only paper. Take a minute or two to write down all the reasons you can't possibly get up earlier, why there is absolutely nothing in the world worth getting up early for, no matter how good it might make you feel, or how much it might benefit you, your family, your friends, your co-workers, or your community...

I can't possibly get up thirty minutes earlier than I currently get up because...

13

Okay, good. Now we have something to talk about.
But before we do, let me share what I wrote three years
ago, when I was [choose any of the following because they
were all true: too lazy, too scared, too comfortable with my
shortcomings] to believe any kind of plan like this could
work. Here are the ~~excuses~~ reasons I came up with then:

I can't possibly get up thirty minutes earlier than I currently
get up because...

I've tried this before and I know it doesn't work. I can't get
up early to do something "good" for me, no matter how hard I
try, no matter how important it seems.

I already get up early enough. Getting up earlier is just going
to piss me off and make me impossible to live with.

If I do this I'll be tired all day and I'll struggle at work.

The sun is in my eye, a rock is in my shoe, and none of the
other kids ever picked me first.

And then a funny thing happened on the way to the truth.
I found out that...

I could get up early "just" to do something good for
myself.

It didn't kill me to get up earlier after all.

And then one day I stopped feeling tired at all.

Of course, you and I are different people, which is why this plan is called **The Fully Automated Treadmill Illumination Plan**, not **The Do What You Feel Like Doing Treadmill Illumination Plan**, or the **If You Think This Will Work For You Please Give It A Try Treadmill Illumination Plan**.

This plan – The Fully Automated Plan – is for people who are willing to admit they might need someone to help them – a friendly coach, a guru, a drill instructor – whoever it takes. This plan is for anyone who has failed at trying to change so many times that they are willing to consider the possibility that they might need a different way of doing things.

Which brings us to a truth you need to face right away. The real reason you are [circle any of the following that apply: overweight, a heavy drinker, a smoker, grouchy, mean spirited, unhealthy, afraid, weak, tired, or generally bored] is because you are either 1) no good at starting a change plan, or 2) no good at sticking with a change plan once you get started. That's okay. Almost no one is – at least not without a little help.

In fact, it's impossible to make changes in your life if you think the change process is overwhelming. What you can do, what anyone can do, is take small steps. This book is a lot of small steps laid out for you. **A Fully Automated Plan**. Not a perfect one, not the only one you will ever need to be happy, but one that will get you started, because ultimately that's what this book is about: **Getting good at getting started on a change plan that will stick** – a different way of doing things.

So for now, imagine a world in which it is possible for you to get up thirty minutes earlier to work a change plan. If you've been paying attention, you know that part of that change plan includes getting on a treadmill. If you're having trouble believing **that will ever happen**, just keep telling yourself this for now –

I can do anything for two days.

Which means you'll need some goals. Because we all know that setting goals is important. We are told that in every school grade. And then we are told it again by our parents and bosses. And then, to make sure we get the point, we are told it ad nauseam for the rest of our lives.

So let's set your goals right now.

Goal 1: Work my change plan two days in a row.

That's it. Exactly one goal. So right now, before you read another word, make a commitment. Make this commitment –

I will get up thirty minutes earlier two days in a row to work my change plan.

Say it out loud several times, with increasing volume.

Say it even if you don't entirely believe it yet.

Say it even if you don't own a treadmill (yes, that's still coming).

But whatever you do, say it with enthusiasm, with passion, as if these are the most exciting and sexy words you'll ever say.

Great! Now let me show you how this all fits together.

You'll work your change plan the first day.

Then you'll work your change plan the second day.

Then you'll take a day off. You'll fluff your feathers like a peacock. You'll thump your chest like a proud silverback. You'll strut your stuff and praise yourself for proving you are a person of your word.

Then you'll work your change plan the first day – again.

Then you'll work your change plan the second day – again.

Then you'll take a couple of days off.

That's it. Get that far and you will have completed the heart of **The Fully Automated Treadmill Illumination Plan**, the engine that makes everything else work. Don't worry, you'll learn the remaining details soon, very important details to be sure, but by committing to take care of working your change plan two days in a row **you have set yourself up so that it will be impossible for you to fail.**

Let's take a minute to celebrate that. If this is true, if you now have a plan that makes it impossible for you to fail, don't you have everything you need to finally feel better about your life? Don't you have everything it takes to shake off that cloud of disinterest that has been following you around for – how long has it been?

But let's get real for a minute. Can a plan this simple really work? Can a plan this easy really lead to happiness? Maybe this is a good time to pause and do a little gut check.

So here it comes, the point when you have to take a leap of faith. And that means you need to do three things before you continue:

1. First, set aside all those naysayer questions swirling through your mind – at least for awhile. Ask them nicely to be quiet. If they don't listen, squash them like an irritating and toxic bug. What are naysayer questions?

   > *Why a treadmill? Why not a stationary bike? Why not a Wii?*
   >
   > *Why does every book like this have to talk so much about "health"?*
   >
   > *Where is all this leading? Why can't you just tell me how all this works so I can get started?*

   I'll answer every one of those questions. Just not right now. Which is kind of the point. Naysayer questions are the kiss of death because they always seem like completely reasonable objections. **In fact, it's naysayer questions that stop you from ever making positive change in your life.** And because we've all been taught to be good questioners, good doubters, good critics, good skeptics, we're very good at coming up with naysayer questions that stop us dead in our tracks.

2. Second, ask yourself a very important question. Before you do, brace yourself. It's the kind of question that requires total honesty, and sometimes total honesty is surprising: **Did you actually think you could change your life without changing who you are?** If you're going to change, you're going to have to change yourself, and that means leaving your comfort zone. Doing new things, going new places, making new friends. Sound a little scary? Then ask yourself this – how much comfort has your comfort zone really been providing?

3. Finally, you need to decide if you trust me, if I'm the kind of person you are willing to have for a personal coach, a completely honest coach who has your best interest in mind. If you haven't done it yet, read this book's introduction, **Who The What?** You'll learn more about me there, plenty to decide.

If after some careful thinking you decide you can't make this kind of leap of faith – at least not with me – there really isn't any point in going on (maybe you can find somebody to "re-gift" your book to).

If making this kind of commitment is something you think you **can** do, this is a great time to move on, because it means you're starting to feel some of the positive energy that comes from making meaningful change. Welcome to your first joy jolt – there are plenty to come.

So since you're sticking around, let's set up a calendar so that your newfound commitment has something real it can be measured against. The easiest way to do that is just like you schedule the rest of your life, by using a calendar built around the days of your work week.

Monday	Tuesday	Wed	Thursday	Friday	Weekend
Work change plan	Work change plan	**DAY OFF**	Work change plan	Work change plan	**2 DAYS OFF**

Simple and clean, but important, because it's easy to see exactly when you work your change plan and exactly when you don't. And it's equally easy to see that **one day off** is not the same as **two days off.** With a commitment calendar there really isn't anywhere to hide.

But there is also something wonderful and magical about your new calendar, something hidden right below the surface.

It's called forgiveness.

It's an understanding that nobody's perfect, that days will be missed, that – unless you never get sick, don't have kids, and never have to travel – you will probably miss entire weeks. So while you need to make a commitment and stick to it –

NEVER LET THIS CALENDAR BECOME YOUR MASTER.

The most important thing is to work your change plan – consistently. So if you miss one day, instead of judging yourself unworthy make up the missed day that weekend, or as soon as you can. To keep yourself from overindulging on forgiveness, keep track of your missed days and the days you make up for them.

Alright, you're almost ready to get started. You have a plan. You have a calendar for working that plan. We still haven't talked about exactly what you'll be doing, but we'll start working on that in the next chapter.

Before we do, let's wrap up this chapter where we started it, by talking about time. If you choose only one thing from this book to commit to that will improve your chances of making your change plan stick, it should be this –

Make the time you work your change plan a time that is completely free from the influence of outsiders.

And the only time of day you really have total control over is the time you wake up earlier than you used to wake up. Think about it. If you used to get up at 6:30 every day to get ready for work, and you now begin waking up at 6:00 to work your change plan, **nothing about your morning will have changed except that 30 extra minutes**.

And because that half hour never existed before, it doesn't really exist now. Your spouse can't lay claim to that 30 minutes, nor can your children, nor your boss, nor any of the important to-dos in your life that otherwise have the power to snatch away your ability to execute a change plan. That thirty minutes is all yours.

If you're thinking you can make some other time of day all yours, be careful. Once your day begins and your life takes on a life of its own, **you lose your ability to control it.** That just means you are a living, vital person with a living, vital life. The only problem with a living vital life is that it thinks for itself, which is not exactly what you're looking for when you need a way to consistently control your time.

What you need is something you can tame **right now** – with total confidence that no one can take control away from you. And the only way you can completely control time is to create time – **to make time out of thin air.**

If this still sounds too painful to consider, keep this in mind. **You don't always have to do things my way.** After you have six months of success under your belt you will be a completely different person, and maybe that person will be able to work his or her plan at a time of his or her choosing. You'll still be taking a chance, but many people do work their plans at times other than the beginning of their day (although most of these people have been at it for awhile).

So if you have a job where you control your own time and you control your environment you might very well be able to work your plan right before lunch each day, or right before you quit each day. That will be great – then – just not now. And, of course, even then, even after you've become strong and sure of yourself, you will always run the risk of losing control of your plan if you lose control of the time when you work it.

So for now, put your trust in the Fully Automated part of this plan. Just reach down into the deepest part of you that really wants to make change work, then agree that maybe the smartest thing for you to do is go along. When you hit your six month anniversary, when you're 20 pounds lighter, when your heartbeat is stronger, when you've decided to take up jogging, when you're celebrating the day you finally quit smoking, when you're calming down and being more productive, send me an email to let me know how you're doing, and either 1) thank me for insisting that you work your plan the first thing every day, or 2) let me know that you'll be sleeping in mornings from now on since you've become a master at working your plan. Either way you'll make me smile.

Before you continue, let me make a suggestion. I'm about to start talking specifics, and that means I'll be asking you to do some work. It might be a good idea for you to read the rest of the book straight through before you start, then you can return to this page and work through one chapter at a time. That way you won't feel any pressure to keep up while you're reading, and you'll be done reading in just a couple of hours. When you return, you'll be ready to use these pages as a friendly guide to help you work your change plan – and you'll know exactly where you're headed!

Chapter 3

Welcome To Your Treadmill

Now that you've agreed to fully automate your change plan, you're ready for your final preparation step – securing a piece of exercise equipment. This step is essential because **The Fully Automated Treadmill Illumination Plan** is based on the scientifically supported fact that –

Happiness is easier to find when you are physically fit.

That means you need a special place to tune up your body while you teach your mind to do the work it needs to do to make you happy.

I highly recommend a treadmill. They're easy to use, and they can be folded up in a corner so that you don't have to look at them all the time. Of course, a stationary bicycle is great, and so is an elliptical machine, a rowing machine, or even one of those long plastic tubs you can swim in without moving. It doesn't really matter what kind of equipment you use, as long as it lets you do all of the following:

1. Get to it every time you need to, at any time of day.

2. Personalize it with a favorite book, an inspiring photograph, or your iThis or iThat.

3. Use it to get in an aerobic workout – which means something good for your heart.

4. Set it up where you'll feel free to talk out loud without feeling like a fool.

This is what my setup looks like.

Nothing fancy, but it works great for me. Why? Because it has everything I need

>1) to feel like I am in my own special place,

>2) to feel at peace, and

>3) to feel successful.

You'll notice I have a tape recorder on hand. It's there so I can capture thoughts to share in books like these, or ideas I have for making a piece of art. I also have a picture of a deep sea turtle right up front, which is there to remind me of my very-longest-term goal. Sometimes I add a new picture, and I often have a stack of books nearby. I wouldn't recommend a television, but if it takes a television to get you on then please add a television today.

If you look closely, you'll also see a piece of paper taped to a piece of cardboard (very chic). This piece of paper is very important, and while I could remove everything else from my workout area and still be successful, this piece of paper is essential to what I do each day to get my mind, my emotions, and my actions to behave the way I want them to. By the time you get rolling, you will have a very attractively mounted piece of paper just like this one of your very own.

Alright, you're ready to get started. I know you don't know all the details of your change plan yet, but that's okay. You've made two very important commitments that will serve you well: 1) you've agreed to work your change plan two days in a row, and 2) you've agreed to use your treadmill as part of your change plan. With those two commitments in place everything else will take care of itself.

All that's left for you to do is –

1. Pick a day when you will begin.
2. Set up your treadmill (or your exercise bike, or your stairmaster; I was kidding about the pool).
3. Say the following as often as you can until your first day arrives: **I can do anything for two days**.
4. When your big day arrives, get up that morning thirty minutes earlier than you normally get up.
5. As soon as you recover from the shock of getting up so early, turn the page and get started.

Congratulations! You are on your way.

Chapter 4

Day 1

Good morning. Before you do anything else – before you eat breakfast or take a shower – please drag yourself, or roll yourself, or walk proudly to your treadmill. Then have a look. You made it, you're here, which means –

You are so far ahead of most people that you have a very good chance of succeeding.

And remember – you only have to do this for two days. So let's get started. Here are your instructions for Day 1. They're not going to change, so they shouldn't take long to memorize.

1. Get on.
2. Turn on your treadmill (it's okay to feel proud, to sing, to smile).
3. Now walk or run until you feel like stopping – then stop.

That's it for Day 1. Really. You have succeeded in launching your change plan.

But if you're like most people, right about now you're wondering if you went far enough. Why? Because you still believe in the importance of goal setting. After all, if you don't have any goals how will you know if you are doing enough to make your change plan work?

Your only goal for this plan – **Work my change plan two days in a row** – says nothing about distances or times or speeds or calories burned because if you get on your treadmill two days in a row, and your neighbor does, and your boss does, and every famous athlete does, and every rich person in the world does, **you all will complete the exact same plan**. It won't matter if you average 15 minutes per workout while your neighbor averages 30. It won't matter if your boss walks slower or faster than you, or if your best friend loses less weight or more. **The only thing that matters is that you work your change plan two days in a row.** If you decide to add distance, or speed, or start running some of the time instead of walking, great. But no one, not even you, needs to know how much, how fast, or how far.

Another reason you should **NOT** set goals for distances, or times, or speeds, or calories burned, is because all of those things are by-products of what you are trying to accomplish – Happiness – but they are not Happiness itself. We all know plenty of very thin or very fast people who would be better off if they learned how to slow down and enjoy a pizza and ice cream with friends.

So at the end of your first day let's make sure this is perfectly clear. **The Fully Automated Treadmill Illumination Plan** is NOT a health plan, it is not a weight loss program, and it is definitely not a contest. **The Fully Automated Treadmill Illumination Plan** is a way to get you on the path to happiness, and it's a way to help you stay there.

But here's some good news about your health anyway. Unless you are a competitive athlete already, you **are** going to get healthier, and you **are** going to lose weight – probably a lot of it. I never set out to lose weight – although I lost 40 lbs – and I didn't care about buying smaller pants – although I knocked six inches off my waist line. My goal was never to quit drinking, but I did, and I certainly didn't care about eating more vegetables, although I do. Why? Because the mind-body link is very real, and the fastest way to a more fit mind is still the tried and true path through a more fit body.

Congratulations again on completing your first workout.

1. You probably lasted a little bit longer than you expected.

2. You are probably more out of shape than you thought.

3. You are probably not all that excited about doing this again.

If I'm wrong about #3 I'm glad, but even if I'm not, never fear. This is where things start to get really interesting, and extremely rewarding.

But first I need you to do a bit of homework tonight.

Chapter 5

Night 1

Question: Which of the following determines a person's ability to be happy?

>   A. Physical Well-Being
>
>   B. Emotional Well-Being
>
>   C. Behavioral Well-Being

If you're scrambling to find where I've hidden *D. All of the above*, you're like most of us, which is interesting, because it shows we have a pretty clear understanding of what it takes to be happy, even if we don't always have the ability to make ourselves happy.

With that in mind, here is your homework for tonight:

1. Write down what **physical well-being** means to you. If you had it, what would you look like? How would you feel?

How much energy would you have? **What would you be able to do physically that you can't do right now?** Write down, word for word, what your best friend would say about you if he or she had not seen you in awhile and ran in to the new physically fit you.

2. Write down what **emotional well-being** means to you. If you had it, how would you feel when you woke up each morning? **What opinion would you have of yourself?** Of others? What emotions would you experience more of than you experience right now? What emotions would you experience less of? Who would you love each day? Who would love you?

3. Write down what **behavioral well-being** means to you. If you had it, what bad habits would you be rid of? What good habits would be new in your life? How would you act when faced with difficult challenges and personal frustration?

Take some time to write your answers down, or if you are more comfortable speaking your answers than you are writing them use a tape recorder to capture your ideas. Whatever you do, don't just speak your answers aloud or think them through in your mind without recording them. Your brain knows when you are serious and when you are pretending.

Okay. You now have everything you need to continue. Tomorrow is Day 2, and we're going to start talking about how you can use your homework answers to start moving your change plan forward in a tangible and meaningful way.

Before we call it a night, take a moment to think about something that too many of us forget to take the time to reflect on – our day-to-day accomplishments.

Your completion rate for this plan is currently 100%.

Right now, you are a person who sticks to his or her commitments, not a quitter.

If you've gotten this far, you have genuine positive momentum.

Just remember to see me bright and early tomorrow morning to keep it up.

Chapter 6

Day 2

Good to see you again. Before you do anything else – before you take a shower, before you eat breakfast – please roll out of bed and make your way to your treadmill.

This should sound familiar, because it's exactly how you began Day 1. Remember, I said your daily instructions would never change:

1. Get on.
2. Turn on your treadmill.
3. Now walk or run until you feel like stopping – then stop.

And because I'm a man of my word, these are indeed your instructions for Day 2. Complete them and you will retain your completion rate of 100%. **Complete them and you will remain way ahead of the game.** In fact, if you keep this up, no matter how far you go each time you're on your treadmill, soon you will notice phenomenal progress, not just physical, but emotional and behavioral as well.

But allow me to make a suggestion. While you are on your treadmill, why not take advantage of your time – that time you fabricated out of thin air – to do something so remarkable that your life will never be the same? What powerful magic am I suggesting?

Teach your brain to think.

First an important distinction – the distinction between your brain and your mind. Your brain is a complex computing tool, a network of neurons, synapses, axons, and dendrites that collects sensory input and takes action based on that input.

For example, your brain, working with your eyes, collects billions of pieces of data, and makes sense of that data, even as you are driving your car at seventy miles per hour through constantly changing traffic. And while your eyes are working with your brain, so, of course, are your hands, arms, feet, and legs, as you steer your car and work the pedals that make your car stop and go. Amazingly, your complex brain is able to compile billions upon billions of pieces of sensory input like this every day, then use that input to instruct your body how to behave to keep you alive and safe.

But your brain is also as dumb as a rock.

It doesn't know the difference between happy and sad, or right and wrong. It doesn't know when you are deluding yourself or when you are actually experiencing a genuine emotion. In fact, your brain has absolutely no idea what you care about, who you want to be, or what contribution you want to make to the world.

Not until you tell it.

Of course, you already tell your brain all sorts of important things, in all sorts of important ways - by being happy, by being afraid, by recoiling physically, by hugging, by honestly confronting loss or by lying about it to avoid pain. All the millions of ways you respond to your experience train your brain - deliberately or without any direction from you - to value certain things more than others.

And as soon as you tell your brain that you value something - even if it's bad for you - your brain will do everything it can to find evidence to support that value.

Your brain, it seems, wants to be helpful.

The good news is that your brain is incredibly flexible. You can take charge of your brain, you can direct it, you can teach it to find only the evidence you want it to find.

So if you want to change yourself - the things you do, the things you say, the habits you have, the way you treat others - you first need a way to direct the evidence that your brain finds for you.

So, let's come back to my suggestion. While you are on your treadmill, why not take advantage of your time – that time you fabricated from thin air to work your change plan – to do something so remarkable that your life will never be the same? And now you know what I'm suggesting, which is –

Why not teach your brain how to think?

If you did your homework last night you have enough to get started, so take out your responses to the three items you wrote about – your physical well-being, your emotional well-being, and your behavioral well-being. Read your responses aloud as you walk or run on your treadmill. Listen for signs of enthusiasm or excitement in your original answers, and amplify that enthusiasm as you speak. Read everything once, then read everything again. And before you stop, read it one more time. If you need to get off your treadmill to finish, go ahead. Then ask yourself this –

Does this new way of looking at the evidence feel better?

You shouldn't expect miracles. Remember, your brain is just beginning to learn how to think. You may not zip through life with a merry smile on your face after just one day, but if you feel some change today, even a slight tingle of how much better it is possible for you to feel, maybe, just maybe, it's worth coming back again after your day off tomorrow.

If you did not do your homework last night, well, do it as soon as you can. You're going to need it for everything else as we move forward. And even if you didn't do your homework, whatever you do, make sure you get on your treadmill today, because everyone needs to come to day three with a 100% completion percentage.

I'll wait for you, no matter how long it takes, so do yourself a favor and get on your treadmill again before you turn the page and start the next chapter.

> **Your brain is about to go on an adventure.**
> **Make sure your body is ready to come along too.**

Chapter 7

Green Marbles And Red Marbles

Days off are the best. Not just because we get to avoid something painful (like early treadmill walks?), but because days off give us time to celebrate our accomplishments. So take a minute to celebrate what you've accomplished so far:

100% completion rate for your treadmill sessions.

Completed 100% of your homework assignments.

Demonstrated an ability to stick with a plan.

Demonstrated an ability to consider a new approach with an open mind.

So while you're feeling good, let's flash back to yesterday for a minute. Let's test the power that reaching different conclusions has to affect how you feel about yourself. For this test, try on the following two conclusions - based on the same experience - to see how they make you feel.

> **Conclusion One:** Big deal. Anyone can complete a schedule that's only two days long and that requires absolutely nothing more from you than standing on a treadmill and turning it on and off. My [mother, brother, friends, co-workers] would laugh out loud if I told them about my "accomplishments."

> **Conclusion Two:** I feel good about what I've done so far, because I know if I can take small steps now and keep taking them I'll be ready to take larger steps later. If my [best friend, sister, neighbor] could hear me now, he [or she] would pat me on the back and buy me a drink.

Here's the interesting thing about these two conclusions. Neither of them is right. And neither of them is wrong.

Not until you tell your brain which one is right for you.

After you do, your brain will know exactly what type of evidence you want it to find: 1) evidence that supports your conclusion that your accomplishments are so small and worthless that your loved ones will mock them, or 2) evidence that supports your conclusion that your genuine effort to move in the right direction is something your loved ones will be proud of.

Which brings us to a great place to be on your day off – a place to start something new. Let's begin with a jar of marbles.

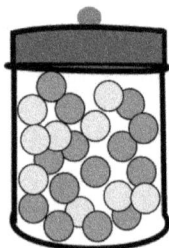

Pretend the jar is you, and that the 100 marbles inside the jar are the conclusions you've reached about your life at any time. To keep things as simple as possible, think of it this way –

Green marbles (shown in light gray) are good because they strengthen your ability to be the kind of person you want to be, while red marbles (shown in dark gray) are bad because they make it harder for you to be who you want to be.

For most of us, the conclusions we reach about our experiences change as events in our lives change, so on a Tuesday you might have 50 green marbles and 50 red in your jar, while later in the week you might have 60 green and 40 red.

But there is something surprising going on here. No matter what is happening in your life you always have a choice to make. You can accept the marbles that are handed to you, or you can learn how to –

Increase the ratio of green to red marbles in your jar.

Consider this example. If you have 40 green marbles in your jar, your ratio of green to red marbles is 40:60, which means that the conclusions in your mind are **50% more negative than they are positive**.

But what would happen if you could change that ratio? What if you had a way to make sure that the majority of your conclusions were green marbles? What if you could change your current ratio of green to red marbles from 40:60 to 75:25? If you could, you would change the conclusions playing in your mind from 50% more negative to **three times more positive**.

That's a life-changing difference.

Make that difference happen consistently and you can go from reaching conclusions like this – *Life is tiring and people annoy me* – to conclusions like this – *I love trying new things and making new friends.*

Let's take a moment to consider what we're talking about practically. If you want to increase your ratio of green to red marbles you have two choices. You can leave things to chance and hope that you are exposed to experiences that produce more green marbles than red ones, or –

You can teach your brain how to find green marbles.

What can you do to help your brain find green marbles and avoid red ones? You can get your brain excited about the hunt.

You can ask questions.

Why questions? Because we are hard-wired to ask questions. We learn by asking questions, and learning is how we stay alive. We ask questions to formulate hypotheses about how the world works, then we conduct tests to find out if our hypotheses are true.

Every time we gently place our hand on something to find out if it is hot, we are asking a question that leads to knowledge. Every time we taste something to find out if we want to eat it, we are asking a question that leads to knowledge. When we try on new clothes, buy a book, ask one person on a date but not another, we are asking questions about the world and looking for answers. Our brains, it seems, love to ask and answer questions.

And it is that affection for questions we're going to take advantage of to find green marbles.

In fact, we are going to dangle questions in front of our brains the way that animal trainers dangle food in front of animals' noses. And when our brains take the bait, they are going to hunt ferociously for the green marbles we need to be happy.

For now, enjoy the rest of your day off.

Chapter 8

Day 1 Again

Good morning, and welcome to Day 1 (again). Here are your instructions.

1. Get on.
2. Turn on your treadmill.
3. Now walk or run until you feel like stopping – then stop.

If you feel like re-reading what you've written about your physical well-being, emotional well-being, and behavioral well-being while walking, please do. Replaying positive conclusions is a great way to stay motivated.

You may remember that on your day off you learned all about green marbles and the power of questions. Tomorrow morning you're going to meet someone who will show you exactly how to use that information to your advantage. For now, savor the satisfaction of doing something you

probably weren't sure you were going to do – stick with a
plan without knowing exactly where you were going.

Your confidence should be growing, and to make sure it is
here is a conclusion you can play in your mind all day.
It should remind you of why you're doing all this –

I am succeeding.

Chapter 9
Day 2 Again

Good morning, and welcome to Day 2 (again). Here are your instructions.

1. Get on.
2. Turn on your treadmill.
3. Now walk or run until you feel like stopping – then stop.

Now allow me to introduce you to someone.

You, I'd like you to meet You.

Okay, that won't work. It's bound to get confusing.
Reminds me a bit of the Monty Python routine where
everyone in the room is named Bruce except for one guy
named Michael, who eventually lets everyone call him Bruce
to avoid confusion. But we won't do that.

Instead, let me tell you about this new you. I'll begin by introducing the two of you a little more distinctly.

You, I'd like you to meet Your Best Possible You.

Not The Perfect You, which is a fantasy, but Your Best Possible You. Not some ephemeral Best Possible You either. I'm talking about a real person, someone as real as you are, although you can't actually touch him.

It's important to know that Your Best Possible You is not an idealized target of who you might become if you do everything perfectly in life. Your Best Possible You is an imperfect human being living in an imperfect world, which makes him just like you and me, which means he makes mistakes – plenty of them. The difference between Your Best Possible You and the you reading these words right now is –

Your Best Possible You already knows what you need to be happy.

I can tell you a few more things about Your Best Possible You without ever meeting him or her.

He enjoys taking care of his body. Exercise is something he looks forward to. He likes paying attention to the things he eats and drinks. He's willing to try yoga or Tai Chi or swimming in fresh water ponds if he learns that those things are good for his body.

She likes taking care of her mind too, and she is as thoughtful about what she feeds her mind as she is about what she feeds her body. She's willing to try reading,

51

puzzle solving, or art at any time in her life.

She enjoys a wide range of emotions – joy, happiness, sadness, loss.

He loves people even if he once forgot that he did.

She likes to do things – act, make a difference, go, move.

I could go on, but I don't want to spoil the fun for you. So before we go any further, let's jump all the way from now to then, to a time in your future when you have become Your Best Possible You.

To help you get there, imagine you are jumping to a specific place, a favorite place, the kind of place Your Best Possible You spends a lot of his or her time. Your special place doesn't have to be somewhere exotic, like a tropical beach (although mine is). It can be a library, a park bench, a waterfall, or a seat in a football stadium, any place that makes you feel good.

Pick carefully though, because you will be spending the entire coming weekend there. The good news is that while you're there you'll be able to do anything you want to do, anything you've ever dreamed of, because you and Your Best Possible You have just won

An all expenses paid weekend getaway to the place of your choosing!

Do anything you like – get a complete work over, water ski, sit in a jacuzzi, sleep, eat, read books, get hammered every night – as long as you agree to come back Monday with everything you need to build your very own change plan (more about that later).

Why go to all the trouble of imagining a favorite place? And why agree to spend a weekend there with an imaginary friend who has a funny sounding name?

Because Your Best Possible You is no more imaginary than you are.

Remember, who you are is determined by the values you have and the conclusions that play in your mind day after day – in other words, by the collection of green and red marbles your brain assembles for you. Your Best Possible You is determined the same way. He or she just has a different collection of marbles. Your goal this weekend – in addition to having as much fun as possible – is to learn everything you can about those marbles.

If you do things right, you'll also make an interesting discovery this weekend. You'll discover how to get rid of persistent bad habits **by literally changing the person who has those habits.** You can finally become [choose any that sound good to you: thinner, more successful, smarter, richer] by trading in the person who is currently [not so thin, not so successful, not as smart as you would like to be, or as rich].

After this weekend you won't have to scour the planet trying to find the person you want to be because you already will have met that person – Your Best Possible You. Make sure you bring your sunscreen, some comfortable clothes, and a pad of paper and a pen.

You're about to be given the answers to your questions before you even know what your questions are.

The truth is funny like that sometimes – sdrawkcab.

Chapter 10

As Good As It Gets

Aloha! Willkommen. Wherever you are, whatever you've decided to do with Your Best Possible You this weekend, welcome.

This Is As Good As It Gets.

You hear that expression a lot, but can you name the events in your life that were as good as it gets? The birth of a child? (that's one of mine.) The day you got married? (another one of mine.) The day you went snorkeling off Little Lameshur and saw a spotted eagle ray ten feet away that was in no hurry to swim off? (yes, another one of mine.)

If you can name even one single time in your life that was as good as it gets, you know that you are a happy person (or can be). If not, I'll trust you to find a way to imagine that kind of day, because for what we're about to do to really work, to "take" as they say, you need to be able to feel the experience of a life moment that is as good as it gets.

Maybe this will help. Remember, you are about to spend two entire days with Your Best Possible You, not The Slightly Improved Version Of You, or The You Who Will Be Happy For A Few Days Then Forget How. This is Your Best Possible You, and believe me, even if you're not entirely convinced yet, Your Best Possible You knows how to be happy.

So get comfortable, slip off your shoes. Turn down the lights, or turn them up. Make yourself a drink or enjoy a glass of water. And don't forget – make sure Your Best Possible You is comfortable too.

Now look.

Closely. Your Best Possible You has your face, but probably doesn't look exactly like you. This doesn't make him a better person than you, or worse. It just means the two of you are different people. Let me give you an example of how this works.

I like to wear jeans, but whenever I bump into My Best Possible You he's wearing nicely pressed khakis. We wear the same kinds of shirts, but that's only because I've started wearing nicer shirts since we met (I've known My Best Possible You for three years now). I would describe My Best Possible You as well dressed, but casual, with just a bit of flare, usually in his shirts.

If noticing how Your Best Possible You looks sounds trivial, it isn't. Your Best Possible You wears clothes that make him feel good about himself, clothes that not only feel good on his body, but honestly reflect the kind of person he is. In other words, Your Best Possible You wears clothes that are consistent with the kind of person he wants to be. You can say the same thing about the jewelry he wears or the way he combs his hair.

So take a moment to notice how Your Best Possible You looks. Go ahead, have a little fun. While you're at it, imagine the clothes he or she wears in the winter too, or if it's winter where you're hanging out try imagining summer clothes. Does Your Best Possible You wear shorts? Makeup? Does Your Best Possible You ever wear white tennis shoes? Loafers? Heels? Combed hair or mussed hair? Tailored shirts or off the rack? Business suits? What kind of tie? When you have a clear picture in your mind – or pictures – you will know the kind of physical appearance that makes Your Best Possible You feel the best about himself or herself.

Now write your answer down so you don't forget it.

Then take a look at something else. Quickly, without really thinking about it, imagine yourself following Your Best Possible You into his home. Smile when he welcomes you inside, then take a look around. Look everywhere. Enjoy yourself. What do you see? How big is the area you are standing in? Anything unusual about where you are? Tall ceiling? No ceiling? Any fountains? Is there artwork on the walls? Can you see outside? Is there furniture nearby? What does the furniture look like? What does the kitchen look like? While you're looking around, be polite. Remember, this isn't your home, it's where Your Best Possible You lives. He or she may have different tastes than you, and he or she might spend more (or less) than you on decorating.

My Best Possible You lives in a house filled with glass and lots of running water, not just fountains, but small rivers. He has very comfortable sofas, but no chairs, and the rooms are very spacious. He likes iron art, like I do, but his tastes are much more modern – white floors and white walls instead of carpet. When I stand in his house I feel energized and happy, and completely at peace with the kind of person I am. I also feel successful.

How do you feel standing inside the home where Your Best Possible You lives?

Write your answer down so you don't forget it.

Whether or not you ever live in this house is unimportant. What matters is that you can see the kind of choices Your Best Possible You has made when it comes to creating the physical space he calls his home.

You can learn a lot about Your Best Possible You by continuing with this kind of visual imagery. After all, most of us are visual creatures, far and beyond any of our other senses. We turn our thoughts and desires into pictures. What do the places Your Best Possible You spends time in look like? Does she hang out at casual coffee shops or at high end wine bars? Does he sit outside in his spare time or hang out in the garage? What does his office look like? Does he even have an office?

You should be able to easily envision Your Best Possible You by now, which is good, because I need you to sit down directly across from him. Yes, at this nice wooden table right behind you. Top off your drinks. Order something to eat.

Then look him right in the eyes and shake his hand.

The two of you should be smiling, because the two of you make each other happy, the way twins almost always enjoy each other's company. Take in the moment. You like her. She likes you. What a beautiful world.

Now talk.

Let your curiosity get the best of you. Be nosy. I can think of lots of questions I'd want to ask right up front...

How did you get so physically fit?

When did you start wearing [pick the item of your choosing]?

Do you still [smoke, drink, swear, swim, hang glide, paint, take pictures, travel]?

Are you married?

Any kids?

What do you do for a living? How much money do you make?

And finally, after you've talked and talked and talked, and after you've finished your meal and your drinks and have started to make small talk, you'll suddenly remember to ask the only question that really matters:

How did you get to be so happy?

Your Best Possible You won't answer right away. After all, you've just gotten to know each other. He doesn't know how much of his story you really want to hear. He doesn't want to say things that make you nervous. He doesn't want to sound like a braggart. But after you sit a few moments in silence he can see that you're serious, and he leans in to answer you.

So listen.

First I figured out what kind of person I wanted to be, then I made a plan for getting there, then I found a tool I could use to help me get there. Then I took my first step, then I took my next step, then I took my next step...

Your Best Possible You lets his words trail off for effect. You smile, but he can see by the slight strain in your smile that you want more than clever story telling. And because Your Best Possible You isn't the kind of person who gives up easily he looks right into your eyes and speaks again.

Let's start by finding out what kind of person you really want to be.

Chapter 11

Who You Want To Be

The sun is getting close to the horizon, but you still have the rest of today and all of Sunday to get this right. So please don't rush. You want to get this right. Your Best Possible You knows you want to get this right too. He even knows you've always wondered if there was a certain kind of person you should be trying to be.

You know the type. Financially successful, yet someone who doesn't really care about money. A person with a plan, but someone who is absolutely spontaneous. Good looking without knowing it, physically fit while still able to enjoy late night pizza and chocolate chip ice cream. You know that part of this doesn't sound quite right, but you are willing to suspend your disbelief.

You feel a cool breeze coming from somewhere, and it feels good. When you take a deep breath the background noise you've been hearing suddenly becomes soothing, like gently folding waves. You wonder if this is part of being The Best Possible You, but before you can ask Your Best Possible You speaks.

"Good," he says. "I'm glad you remembered to bring a pen and some paper."

You feel a little flare in your stomach, but then you remember that Your Best Possible You is on your side so this isn't likely to be a test.

"So let's figure out who you want to be," he says, as if this little challenge is like building a model airplane together, or doing one of those paint by number pictures.

In fact, you may have thought about doing something like this before, then wondered if you had the [pick one: imagination, fortitude, resolve] to get it done. Despite your doubts about succeeding now, when you look up it's hard to miss the obvious proof that you can get at least part of the way there on your own. Your Best Possible You is sitting right across the table from you. You've even been inside his home. If you can conjure an entire house and the person who lives in it from nothing, is it really such a stretch to believe you can figure out what makes that person tick?

Still, you wouldn't mind a few ground rules.

"We'll keep things simple," Your Best Possible You says, and you realize what a relief it's going to be not to have to explain every little thing you're thinking. "We'll come up with a list of behaviors you'd like to adopt instead of specific outcomes."

You're not sure you entirely understand, so you make that face you make when you are uncertain about something but don't want to appear slow. Your Best Possible You picks up on your visual cue.

"Instead of saying 'I'll never lose my temper again,' you can say something like 'I'd like to live a calm and peaceful life.' Or, you might say something like 'I want to be satisfied with whatever work I do to earn money,' instead of 'I want to get rich.'"

You smile but you're a little bit disappointed. You would love to never lose your temper again, and being rich would solve more than one or two of your problems. Still, you decide to keep going.

"This will be a lot easier once I know the things that really matter to you."

At this you sit up, take notice, and smile. You have a surprise for Your Best Possible You, something you can give him that will help him learn a lot about what matters to you. In fact, you have three things.

The first thing you have is your description of what **physical well-being** means to you. But before you give it to him, take a few minutes to revise what you've written. Go ahead. Make it shine. Make it more exciting, snappier. Live large, dream bold. Imagine exactly what you look like. How you feel. How much energy you have. Visualize all the things you can do physically that you can't do right now. And don't forget, you have a word-for-word description of what your best friend would say about you if he or she had not seen you in awhile. Make sure you give that to Your Best Possible You too.

The second thing you have is your description of what **emotional well-being** means to you. If you need to, take a few minutes to revise what you've written. Make it as honest as you can. Reach closer to your heart. Write a powerful description of the humble but positive opinion you have of yourself, and of others. Write down the emotions you want to experience more of, and less of, than you experience now. Describe your relationships with the people who matter most to you in life.

The final thing you have for Your Best Possible You is your description of what **behavioral well-being** means to you. Feel free to revise what you've written. Transform yourself into a brave new thinker. Challenge yourself to new heights. Write about the ways you behave from day to day that please you, and about the ways you behave that absolutely have to change. Describe things you do that you are proud of.

Once you feel completely comfortable with what you've written, slide it across the table.

Then wait.

There's a good possibility that Your Best Possible You is patient, so resist the temptation to rush him. He is probably the kind of person who wants to get things right before he rushes off following the wrong plan. If he laughs or chuckles, don't worry that you've said something to embarrass yourself. Your Best Possible You most likely has a good sense of humor, which means he understands that laughing at ourselves is a sign of good mental health.

If things have gone well – and if you've supplied Your Best Possible You with honest descriptions of your different types of well-being there really is no reason to think things will go any other way – when Your Best Possible You finishes reading what you've written he will sit back in his chair and smile.

"This is going to be easy," he'll say. "You've already done the hard part."

You smile, but feel uneasy. You're not in love with every word you've written, and some of your descriptions seem a bit vague.

"Don't worry," Your Best Possible You finally says. "I'm going to show you how to turn this into magic."

You laugh, and you're genuinely thankful for his unbridled optimism, but deep down inside you're not sure you believe in magic. You remember those times you've gotten this far before then had everything get derailed. You take this moment to remind yourself that reality is, after all, reality.

You look to Your Best Possible You for help, but he's already thinking about something else. You begin to wonder if you've put your trust in the right person, or if Your Best

Possible You might have had too much of the island punch to drink.

"I know what you're thinking," Your Best Possible You says, and you know that he must. How else could he have gotten from where you are to where he is without having the same doubts.

"But your problem isn't really figuring out who you want to be. You have everything you need right here for that. You might not have worked out every little detail yet, but you know exactly who you want to be physically, emotionally, and behaviorally."

You start to smile, but then you feel that uneasy feeling in your stomach again. Knowing is one thing, doing another, and even if you know who you want to be you still need a plan for getting from here to there.

But Your Best Possible You is clearly at ease, and for some reason you don't completely understand his easiness makes you decide to do something you're not always good at. You decide to trust.

"And now for the magic," Your Best Possible You says.

And with that he spins around the descriptions you've written so that both of you can see them at that same time.

And then he starts writing.

Where you've written something like...

My PHYSICAL WELL-BEING

I have energy all the time now.

I look 5 years younger than I really am.

I run In weekend races with my family.

I lift weights three times a week.

I'm ten pounds lighter and still losing weight!

I sleep soundly every night.

If my best friend from high school saw me he would Probably say "You look great. Did you join a gym or something?"

Your Best Possible You writes...

What will I experience today that gives me plenty of energy to do the things I care about?

What experience will I have today that reminds me that how old I am is largely up to me?

What will I do today that reminds me how good it feels to move around and exercise?

What will I notice today to remind me that it feels good to be getting rid of those extra pounds?

How many times today will I notice how much better I feel now that I sleep better?

You nod after you read the final question. You want Your Best Possible You to think you're evaluating the questions he has written objectively, the way people are supposed to evaluate new ideas.

But inside, where no one is watching, you're a fountain of hope. And you recognize this feeling, although you probably don't remember from when or where, this feeling that you've just been shown something with the power to change.

"So here it is," Your Best Possible You says. "Your moment of truth. Which means you probably want all this explained. We can do that if you want, we can take more time to talk, but I have a much better idea."

And very slowly, as if his deliberateness is part of his persuasive appeal, he slides your list of descriptions directly in front of you, then places your pen gently on top.

"Why don't you take it out for a test drive? **My Emotional Well-Being** looks ready to go. Come to think of it, **My Behavioral Well-Being** looks eager too."

When you look down at the page you see that you're already holding your pen.

Your Best Possible You glances at his watch, then stands up. "I have to warn you, I'm an early riser. The good news is I'm also a fairly decent cook. So I'll see you in the morning?"

You nod, then just like that you find yourself alone at the table. You try to settle in to think, but before you can lean all the way back you have an overpowering urge to write.

So write.

My Emotional WELL-BEING

What will I experience today that...

Chapter 12

Getting There, Part One

What a beautiful Sunday morning. You definitely picked a great place to spend a weekend. By the way, Your Best Possible You is already up and waiting in the kitchen (he's probably already worked out this morning too). When you step out of your room, you see that he is dressed in casual sweats, but looks as if he could go directly from here to a gallery opening or a museum without needing to change.

"I can't remember how you take your coffee," he says, which almost makes you laugh, but then you realize that how you take your coffee might have nothing to do with how he takes his coffee.

When he pours, you see that he also takes his coffee [black, with cream, as tea]. For some reason this makes you smile, which Your Best Possible You seems to pick up on.

"I like keeping some things the way they've always been," he says.

This is a big relief, because last night as you re-read your list of questions one last time before leaving them on the kitchen table, some of them seemed lackluster. In fact, there are a few places you got completely stuck. You even found yourself wishing that Your Best Possible You had taken some of that time he offered to explain how everything works. Now you're worried that Your Best Possible You will read your questions and think you unambitious, or worse, shallow.

You sit down, look out the window, then start talking about the weather, but Your Best Possible You doesn't seem interested. You try talking about [sports, current events, movies, books] but the more you talk the less interested Your Best Possible You seems.

"Something the matter?" you ask.

When Your Best Possible You pulls your list of questions from beneath a folded newspaper you see that the paper you wrote on the night before is covered with red ink, the way graded school papers used to look before teachers finally figured out that red ink isn't all that inspiring.

"I took some liberties," Your Best Possible You says.

It's hard to see any evidence of what you wrote under all that red, especially all the way across the table. But the biggest surprise of all is finding out that all that red ink doesn't really bother you. That kind of criticism used to make your confidence rush out of you like water spouting from a can riddled with quarter-sized holes.

"Interesting, isn't it?" Your Best Possible You asks. "Last night you wrote a question that says," and here he holds your paper up to see better, "'What will I experience today that make me confident in my abilities?' and this morning, even after you've been ambushed with an ocean of red you remain confident."

He spins the page toward you, then smiles. "Besides, I was just having some fun. Everything looks great."

When you pull the page toward you you see that he has written the same thing up and down the page in red.

Time to get started!

And like that you are off to change the rest of your life. Almost. Before you can say anything, Your Best Possible You picks up a water bottle and heads for the front door.

"Where are you going?"

"Bike ride. It's new for me and I'm loving it. There are some nice trails not too far away. I'd ask you to come, but – "

"What ever happened to *Let's figure out who you want to be?*"

"Didn't we do that last night?"

You look at your questions and realize that Your Best Possible You is right. Still, things are not as tidy as you would like them to be. You have a pretty good idea of the person you would like to become, but the only thing you have – the only thing you can touch – is a bunch of words on paper. "I guess I was hoping you'd help me figure out how to get from here to there."

Your Best Possible You drops his keys on the table, then sits down.

"I can do that," he says, "but – "

You grimace, awaiting the usual "you'll feel better if you do this yourself" sentiment.

Then he surprises you. "Have you ever heard of a book called **The Fully Automated Treadmill Illumination Plan**?"

You shake your head. With a title like that you'd remember.

"Sometimes it's called **The Bright Red Book of Happiness**."

This rings a bell, but you don't really have time to say anything. Your Best Possible You takes a deep breath, then dives right in. You listen carefully, and as you listen you get that overpowering feeling of déjà vu.

"According to the book, when you ask questions your brain searches the world high and low for evidence that supports whatever it thinks you are asking it to find. Ask 'why are people so lousy?' and your brain will deliver evidence of lousy people doing lousy things to prove you right. Ask 'where can I meet people who inspire me?' and suddenly inspirational people will appear everywhere – courtesy of your hard-working brain."

The feeling of déjà vu is overwhelming now, and you almost feel like asking Your Best Possible You to stop. But he continues.

"The book says if you want to get from here to there the secret is figuring out the right questions to ask. Once you have them, you dangle them in front of your eager-to-please brain like an animal trainer dangling food in front of a hungry animal. Over, and over, and over again."

You wish you were rich so you could give Your Best Possible You every penny you had ever earned to write out the rest of your questions for you – word for word. You're still not sure what to do with abstract desires like peace of mind and inner strength. When he grimaces a bit, you can see that he is onto you.

"Look, I know it's powerful to jump from where you are to where you want to be, and it's powerful for us to talk this way, but for all of this to work you have to take all the steps in between on your own. Last night you made a great start on the questions you need to get there. Why not take the rest of today to get them just right? If you can do that, I have one more piece of magic to share."

You nod and point to his keys on the table.

"Enjoy your ride."

Your Best Possible You grabs his keys and stands up.

"Before I go, I have a little present for you." He reaches

inside his folded newspaper, then pulls out a sheet of paper. "No one ever said that doing things for yourself meant you had to do them entirely alone."

He slides the paper toward you, then steps out the door.

And this is what you see.

Quality you want to possess (see your physical, emotional, and behavioral lists).	Green marble you need to find to help you develop that quality.	Question to dangle in front of your brain to make it hunt for that green marble.
Exercise consistently.	Anything that makes me believe that exercise is not torture.	What will I discover today that makes me enthusiastic about doing something fun to exercise?
Be optimistic about my future.	Evidence that it's possible to feel great in a great world (or at least a pretty good world).	What will happen today to fuel my optimism that the world is a great place, and that my future in it can be great too?
Act calmly even when things get crazy around me .	People who remain calm even when they're working in chaotic environments.	Who will I learn about, or who will I meet, who has mastered the art of remaining calm in the eye of the storm?

Chapter 13
Good-byes

Even in imaginary lands with imaginary friends weekends end, and this one is rapidly approaching its final moments. Your Best Possible You, up early again, is already packed and standing by the front door on this bright and shiny Monday morning.

"Where are you off to?" you ask, and Your Best Possible You grins.

"Wouldn't you like to know?"

Yes, you would like to know exactly how Your Best Possible You spends his time, but after spending yesterday writing [10, 15, 20] questions about green marbles that you're proud of, you're content to let your future arrive when it's ready.

Still, you are not quite ready to say good-bye. There is something you need to ask, and Your Best Possible You still owes you a final piece of magic.

"When am I supposed to ask my brain all these questions?"

Your Best Possible You smiles, then opens the door.

"Do you remember that book I told you about?"

"The one about the bright red treadmill?"

"That's the one." Your Best Possible You laughs, then hands you a piece of paper. "Here's that final piece of magic," he says, then he steps through the door.

"It's been – Well, I guess I shouldn't say 'real,'" he says, then laughs.

You walk out right behind him but he's already gone.

In your hand you hold a piece of paper. Look at it.

Read The Bright Red Book Of Happiness, Ch. 14, "Getting There, Part Two."

Chapter 14
Getting There, Part Two

Good morning, and welcome to Day 1 (for the third time).

Here's something encouraging to consider –

You are four workouts ahead of yourself if you had decided to wait until today to start working your change plan.

And, of course, you're infinitely ahead of yourself if you had made an entirely different decision, say, for example, **not** to put any effort into a change plan at all. If you think about that for a few minutes you'll discover something **very** encouraging –

You are already becoming a different person, the kind of person who works change plans and sticks to her decisions.

Nice work!

Here are your instructions for today.

1. Get on.
2. Turn on your treadmill.
3. Now walk or run until you feel like stopping – then stop.

I almost forgot. Welcome back! I hope you had an enjoyable weekend. I'm sure you learned a lot about yourself, and I trust you've returned with everything you need to work your change plan.

If you've put in a good faith effort, you should have a list of questions you're pretty happy with. Now it's time for you and me to work together to help you ask those questions at just the right time to get you where you want to be.

Before we do, it seems only right for me to share something with you – the exact questions I use to work my personal change plan. After all, I've asked you to do a lot of self examination, and at each step of the way I've urged you to be both honest and brave. Now it's time for me to be as brave with you as I'm asking you to be with yourself.

I should tell you that I've changed my questions no fewer than four times during the last three years, and sometimes I've added story-like paragraphs to motivate myself. I have, however, been dangling the same set of core questions in front of my brain since Day 1. Those are the first six questions on my list.

Without further adieu...

GETTING READY FOR THE DAY

Emotionally

1. What can I do or experience today that will make me happier and more optimistic?

2. What can I see or experience today that will add beauty to my life?

Physically

3. What can I do or experience today to continue making healthy choices?

4. What can I do or experience today to continue choosing to be a non-drinker?

Behaviorally

5. What will happen today to help me easily be calm?

6. What can I do or experience today that will help me model calm, confident behavior for my daughter?

GETTING PRIMED FOR ACTION

7. What can I do today to easily select the most important thing to work on right now?

8. What can I do today to work diligently from end to end?

9. What will I do today to get better at completing things easily and quickly?

10. Who will I meet today that is interesting and inspiring?

GETTING THERE, PART TWO

There you have it. Nothing fancy, and nothing so difficult that you shouldn't be able to imagine doing this for yourself.

Still, don't underestimate the power of these questions. Each and every day I ask them I take advantage of my brain's fascination with finding answers to get my brain to work for me, which leaves me free to do the things I love doing.

And look at everything I get my brain to help me do each day just by asking these questions:

Meet people who inspire me, which encourages me to do meaningful things with my life.

Push the envelope of optimism to make myself a genuinely happy person.

Stop to smell the roses, hear the birds sing, watch the children laugh, and notice the beautiful light that illuminates the world.

Live a healthy life so that I'm here as long as possible to share it with the people I love.

Be calm and confident so that my daughter learns to be calm and confident too.

Easily figure out which work to do from the endless possibilities that any job and any life present.

Work each day without losing my enthusiasm for what I'm doing.

Produce results in a short period of time, without having to feel as if I'm working in a frenzy.

Make art that is brave and interesting.

These are the things that matter to me. Some of them may be things that matter to you. In fact, some of our questions might be identical, although it's important for your questions to direct your brain to find those personal green marbles that are just right for you.

Alright. You've seen my questions and you have your own questions. We still have something we need to figure out.

When are you supposed to ask all these questions?

You're already getting up early to get on your treadmill two days in a row, so I wouldn't dream of suggesting that you get up any earlier, or that you stay up later, or that you "squeeze" asking your questions into time slots that are probably already overflowing with things to do.

Instead, I'm going to make a simple suggestion. Why don't you let me make a slight change to your daily instructions? Something like this:

Here are your instructions for today.
1. Get on.
2. Turn on your treadmill.
3. Now walk or run until you feel like stopping
   – then stop. **While you are walking or running, ask yourself your daily questions.**

Before you call me a liar and a cheat (after all, I did say your instructions would never change), let me point out a few things that I hope will persuade you to forgive me:

1. Sooner or later you're going to discover that having nothing else to do while walking on a treadmill can get a bit boring, especially as you get stronger and feel like spending more time on your treadmill (something that almost always happens). If you don't have something to do to help pass the time you increase the chance that you will abandon your plan altogether – the ultimate disaster.

2. I am not normally a big fan of "multi-tasking," but the task of walking on a treadmill and the task of asking questions have almost nothing to do with each other. One is an entirely physical task; one is entirely mental. There is no reason to think you would get more out of your walk, or more from asking your questions, if you performed only one of those tasks at a time. This makes your time on the treadmill a perfect time to multi-task.

And there is another good reason to ask your questions while walking –

Tasks performed while you invigorate your body have very high rates of "taking" success.

In other words, the more invigorated your body is when you ask your questions the more likely your brain is to find the green marbles you need.

Or you can think about this at the sensory level. An invigorated body has supercharged senses, including

85

hearing, vision, and speech. If you read your daily questions while you are walking or running, **you will actually see your questions better**. And because your vision is hyper-activated, you will actually read your questions with better clarity than you do when you are not on your treadmill.

Now imagine what happens if you read your questions aloud. Your hyper-activated sight turns the words you read into hyper-activated sounds that form words for your hyper-activated ears to hear, then send to your hyper-activated mind to make sense of.

With all that energy going around, it seems a shame not to take advantage of it. Why not go ahead and upgrade your daily instructions? The only change you're really making is to do something during the time you were already doing something else.

That's it for now. Our goal from the beginning has been to give you a fully automated change plan that helps you [choose all three: 1) get started, 2) stick with it, 3) make changes]. You have that plan now, and you have the questions you need to make that plan work.

Just remember –

> **You can do anything for two days – even something a little extra.**

Chapter 15

What To Expect Since You're Expecting

Good morning, and welcome to Day 2 (for the third time).

Here are your instructions for today.

1. Get on.
2. Turn on your treadmill.
3. Now walk or run until you feel like stopping – then stop. While you are on, ask yourself your daily questions.

Now that we have that all locked down – the steps you will follow and how often you will follow them – you are probably wondering what you can expect from your new change program.

Believe me, this one is tempting. The scientific, analytical, rational thinking Westerner in me really wants to take a stab at describing the changes you will experience during your first three months, your first six months, and then again at

that wonderful but totally meaningless sign post called
One Year.

But then I remembered that none of that matters.

If you are now on a course that will result in your losing
ten pounds or forty, in one year or two, why do you need to
know anything in advance? If you are finally about to quit
[choose anything], or if you are finally about to start [choose
anything else], or if you are finally about to lighten up or
bear down, why do you need to know so much about how
much, when, and how well?

The painful truth is that Westerners, at least Americans, are
way too worried about things like time lines, measurement
by objectives, and outcome-based learning because we are
way too worried about success, which is amusing since so
few of us seem to understand what success really means.

If we did, why would we read so many books like this
one? (myself included)

In the end, you have to believe that change is good for its
own sake, that if change is undertaken because you want to
enjoy life or feel better about yourself **that the outcomes of
enjoying and feeling better are good enough.**

Does that mean you should never stop to examine what you
are doing? No. It means that you should examine the success
of your change plan according to your own standards, and
by now I would imagine you know where to find those
standards.

They are embedded within the questions you ask yourself.

For example, when I want to know how I'm doing, when I want to evaluate my change plan according to my own standards, I ask myself the following:

Am I....

Feeling more optimistic and happier?

Stopping to smell the roses, hear the birds sing, watch the children laugh?

Living a healthy life?

Acting calmly?

Meeting people who inspire me?

Making art that is brave and interesting?

Of course, this is how I examine **my** change plan – based on **my** standards. You should examine your change plan based on standards embedded in **your** questions. Your answers will tell you where you are doing well, and where you need more work, perhaps by revising some of your questions.

If you stick with your plan I **can** tell you this about the future.

You are going to be surprised, perhaps even astonished, at every single checkpoint you set up for yourself.

To prove my point, I'll illustrate how far I've come following the one simple rule I've asked you to follow – **Work my change plan two days in a row.**

> **HEALTH**: I weigh the same as the day I graduated from high school. If double knit pants, silk shirts, and platform shoes were still in style I could wear the same clothes today that I graduated in. My blood pressure, cholesterol, and every other health number look great.

> **HABIT CHANGE #1**: It's been more than six years since I've smoked or used nicotine. I got that rolling before I started this plan, but this plan has helped me reach a place where I no longer desire nicotine. In fact, if they proved tomorrow that smoking was good for you I wouldn't start again.

> > And now I'm going to take a moment to flat out preach – **If you smoke you must find a way to quit.** If you don't, you will die a painful death, and you will torture every one of your loved ones along the way.

> **HABIT CHANGE #2**: It's been almost three years since I've had an alcoholic drink, and this is an idea I tossed in just to discover where it might lead. I now enjoy waking up each morning knowing exactly what I will get from myself.

> **PERSONAL DEVELOPMENT**: My art is going better than ever. I make things now that I did not know I could make, like painted plates, and bamboo backed tile art,

and art made from bed springs. I write better, I take better pictures, and all of it is easier and more fun than it has ever been.

MENTAL HEALTH: As I write these words I am happier, lighter of spirit, more focused, more productive, and more glad to be alive than I have ever been.

That last one alone should convince you to stick with your plan as long as you can.

One last thing: There are plenty of great books out there to keep you company – inspiring books about inspiring people and inspiring ways to think. I read them constantly, learning as I go. While you are on your way to great things, why not look for a few friends to keep you company on the way?

For now, keep it fully automated.

Chapter 16

What Might Be Possible

It's a beautiful morning. The sky is full of sunlight that strikes everything in just the right places, in just the right amounts, a photographer's dream. Even brand new photographers can take prize-worthy photos on a day like this because the sun has done all the work.

Ordinary tree branches remind you of slender graceful arms. Flat-faced concrete buildings remind you more of watercolor washes than places where people go to work. Each time you turn your head to look at something new that perfect light seems to follow you, and you begin to wonder if your eyes are deceiving you. After all, you would have noticed light like this before. Wouldn't you?

What can I do or experience today to help me take in more of the beauty that surrounds me?

That evening you're enjoying dinner at your favorite restaurant with your [wife, husband, girlfriend, boyfriend] when you look up and see a little girl about five years old smiling at you. You smile back, then make a funny face, which makes the child laugh, which makes her mother laugh, which makes your [wife, husband, girlfriend, boyfriend] smile, which, of course, makes you smile. You wonder if maybe it's just you, or if everyone around you suddenly seems happier now.

What will I do or discover today that helps me make others happy?

Later that night, you're at a party, listening to one of your co-workers describe the new business she has decided to start. You hear her say things like **the sky's the limit** and **you only have one life to live**. Of course, you've heard expressions like this before, but suddenly they sound like advice.

What will I do or experience today that renews my belief in the possible?

At the end of the night, when you go to get your jackets, you see a white rose in a slender vase – light striking the rose in just the right places.

What's going on here? What makes this kind of day possible?

Your mind reaches thousands of conclusions about your life every day, and those conclusions determine what you do with the rest of your life. The good news is that your mind wants to help, and it's forgiving. Even if you've neglected it for years, all you have to do is ask it to help and it will learn to remember that almost anything is possible.

- Would you like to notice that perfect light instead of driving right through it?

- Would you like the courage to try new things?

- Would you like your children to remember you as a supportive parent who smiles and laughs and hugs and encourages?

- Would you like to have days when you feel as good as you felt when you were a child riding your bike down a long steep hill just because the wind on your face felt good?

What will I experience today that makes me feel completely alive?

There are [hundreds, thousands, millions] of people out there who want to ride down that hill with you. Some of them are ready to go right now. Others need a nudge.

We're all in this together, so it's up to us what we do with the ride. We can soar down the hill together, or we can sit at the top of the hill and wonder.

Let's ride!

Working Your Change Plan

Get On The First Time

☑
☐
☐

Get On Again

☐
☐
☐

Teach Your Brain To Think

☐
☐
☐

Hunt For Green Marbles

☐
☐
☐

Meet Your Best Possible You

☐
☐
☑

Lead The Way With Questions

Appendix

Questions You Can Use Right Now

Because this book features a **Fully Automated** plan, it seems only right to leave you with questions you can use right now. With that in mind, the questions that follow are ready for you to lift, tweak, and use. Don't worry about finding perfect questions. Sometimes it helps just to take the first questions that jump out at you. You can always change what you have later.

As you prepare your list of questions, look for two or three in each of the first three areas, then maybe a few from **The Board of Specific Change Questions** (a few pages ahead) that apply to you. Whatever you do –

Keep your final list to less than one page.

Questions to Ask about Physical Well-Being

What will happen today to help me discover that exercise is actually fun?

What book or article or story will I read today to get me excited about taking care of my body?

What will I experience or do today to help me eat right?

What will I experience or do today to feel good about deciding not to drink as much (or at all)?

What picture of healthy people will I see today that inspires me to stick with my exercise plan?

What new foods can I try today that are good for me?

What can I learn today about nutrition that will make it fun to pay attention to what I eat?

Who will inspire me to take good care of myself today?

What will I do today so that when I go to bed I can say *At least I did that today to take care of my body?*

Questions to Ask about Emotional Well-Being

What will I do or experience today that makes me optimistic?

What will I do or experience today that makes me happy?

What will happen today to make me smile?

What will happen today to make me laugh?

What will I see or experience today that adds beauty to my life?

What will I do today that reminds me that I like people?

Who will I meet today that I feel connected to?

What will I do today so that when I go to bed I can say *At least I did that today to feel good emotionally?*

Questions to Ask about Behavioral Well-Being

What will I do or learn today to start taking care of things as soon as they need to get taken care of?

What will I do today to help me become more patient?

What can I do or experience today to help me avoid frustration and anger?

What will I experience today that helps me [fill in the blank] more?

What will I experience today to make it easier for me to [fill in the blank] less?

Who will I meet today whose actions I can learn from?

Who will I meet today who inspires me to act the way I want to act?

What will I do today so that when I go to bed I can say *At least I did that today to act the way I wanted to?*

The Board of Specific Change Questions

People	Habits	Doing	Goals
What will I experience today to help me be a better [parent, spouse, partner]?	What can I do or learn today to reinforce my decision not to [fill in the blank] anymore?	What can I learn today to help me work faster?	What will I do or learn today to find new opportunities for financial security?
What can I do today to meet new and inspiring people?	Who will I meet that inspires me to stick to my commitment not to [fill in the blank] anymore?	What can I experience today that makes me more productive?	What will I experience today that makes it easy for me to invest wisely for the future?
What can I do or learn today to be less judgemental?	What can I learn or experience today that makes it easy for me to start [fill in the blank]?	What can I experience today that helps me work without distraction?	What will I learn or do today that moves me closer to my goal of [fill in the blank]?
What can I do or learn today to uplift others?	What surprising thing will I learn today that helps me start doing [something rewarding]?	Who will I meet or learn about today that makes it easy for me to learn a new skill?	Who will I meet today that inspires me to reach my goal of [fill in the blank]?
What will happen today that makes me act kindly?		What can I learn or do today that makes work easier and more satisfying?	What new technique or strategy will I uncover today that helps me [blank]?

About The Author

Philip Deal lives with his wife and daughter in North Carolina. He has taught writing at Wichita State University, Georgia Southern University, and at several technical colleges.

Want to read another book by this author?
Love In An Iron Bowl is now available to order online. You can also read free samples from **Love In An Iron Bowl** at philipdealbooks.com